GUARDIAN K9s ON A MISSION

Book 1: K9 Preacher

Written by
Billye Survis

Illustrated by
Lynne Lillge

Paperback ISBN-13: 978-1-957351-81-0

GUARDIAN K9s ON A MISSION | Book 1 - K9 Preacher
Written by Billye Survis | Illustrated by Lynne Lillge
Edited by Griffin Mill | Layout by Michael Nicloy

Published by Nico 11 Publishing & Design
Mukwonago, Wisconsin
www.nico11publishing.com

Be well read.

Quantity orders may be placed with the publisher via email:
mike@nico11publishing.com

Printed in The United States of America

To Jessie and Tiffany,

Your work moves us forward, inspires us, and reminds us why we do what we do. "Thank you" will never be enough, but I say it with the deepest gratitude and respect. This book is dedicated to you-your service, your sacrifice, and your relentless pursuit of making a difference.

FOREWORD

Service dogs have long played a vital role in assisting military personnel, veterans, first responders, and Gold Star families, providing not only companionship but also essential support in overcoming physical and emotional challenges. These highly trained K9s serve as unwavering partners, offering comfort, security, and life-changing assistance to those who have sacrificed so much for our communities and country.

Wisconsin Guardian Foundation (WGF) is dedicated to ensuring these heroes receive the support they deserve. As a 501(c)(3) nonprofit, WGF operates solely for charitable purposes, with a mission to serve and uplift U.S. military members, veterans, first responders, and Guardian Honor families. Completely run by volunteers, WGF ensures that 100% of proceeds go directly into funding programs that provide life-changing services, including the placement and of highly trained service dogs for those in need.

The books in this series are a tribute to the incredible impact of K9 service dogs—their intelligence, loyalty, and ability to transform lives. Through the unwavering support of organizations like WGF, these specially trained dogs continue to offer hope, independence, and healing to those who have given so much.

If you are inspired by our mission and would like to learn more, seek assistance, or support our cause, we invite you to visit www.wiguardianfoundation.org. Your contribution—whether through awareness, donation, or direct involvement—helps us continue providing vital programs and resources to those who need them most.

Thank you for joining us in honoring and supporting our nation's heroes.

With gratitude,

WI Guardian Foundation

PREACHER

Hi, my name is Preacher and I'm so excited. Today is going to be the best day ever!

All of my life I knew I wanted to help people, but not just anybody, I wanted to help heroes.

To help me get ready, my family made sure I got lots of training when I was growing up.

I went to lots of different places to get used to different noises and smells.

I went to the grocery store...

I went to the hardware store...

I went to the park...

I met lots of other dogs, animals, and people so I would know how to behave.

Finally, when I was about
two-and-a-half years old
(that's about 28 years old in human years!),
I got a call that a hero needed my help!

My hero, Jessie, is an Army Veteran and former police officer and Marine Corps K9 trainer.

I hopped on the first plane I found, but before I could help my hero, I needed to get some special training to take care of him.

Jessie helps keep police officers safe by training my fellow dogs to be their partners, helpers, and protectors. How cool is that?

After I got off the plane in Wisconsin, I went through my own training so I knew how to help Jessie.

I learned how to pick up lots of
different things to bring to him.

I can even bring
him his car keys!

I learned how to tell if hero Jessie needs me to comfort him, I lean in on his legs and give him a big doggie hug to let him know everything is alright. I also learned that sometimes people are too close to him and he needs some space. I just let out a couple of loud barks to tell people to give him some room.

Next up, I get to move in with hero Jessie, his wife Tiffany, and their kids. I get to live with all of them!

I can't wait to
meet my new
best buddy and
help my hero!

Thank you Wisconsin Guardian Foundation and Jessiffany Canine Services for helping dogs like me help heroes like Jessie.

www.ingramcontent.com/pod-product-compliance
Lightning Source LLC
Chambersburg PA
CBHW040850120626
46547CB00001B/102